The Homeric Hymn to Demeter

By

Homer

Translated from the Greek by

Hugh G.Evelyn-White

First published in 1914

Published by Left of Brain Books

Copyright © 2023 Left of Brain Books

ISBN 978-1-397-66902-5

First Edition

All rights reserved. No part of this publication may be reproduced, distributed, or transmitted in any form or by any means, including photocopying, recording, or other electronic or mechanical methods, without the prior written permission of the publisher, except in the case of brief quotations permitted by copyright law. Left of Brain Books is a division of Left Of Brain Onboarding Pty Ltd.

PUBLISHER'S PREFACE

About the Book

"In Greek mythology Dêmêtêr ("mother-earth" or possibly "distribution-mother" from the noun of the Indo-European mother-earth *dheghom *mater) is the goddess of grain and fertility, the pure nourisher of the youth and the green earth, the health-giving cycle of life and death, and preserver of marriage and the sacred law. She is invoked as the "bringer of seasons" in the Homeric hymn, a subtle sign that she was worshipped long before the Olympians arrived. Another story states that she was one of the twelve Olympians. The Homeric Hymn to Demeter has been dated to sometime around the Seventh Century BC. She and her daughter Persephone were the central figures of the Eleusinian Mysteries that also predated the Olympian pantheon.

The Roman equivalent is Ceres, from whom the word "cereal" is derived."

(Quote from wikipedia.org)

About the Author

"Homer, the greatest name in this history of epic poetry, and who stands as high in that department as William Shakespeare does in the drama, has come down to us in modern times unfortunately as little better than a name, and presents materials for biography as scanty as those which he offers for criticism are rich. We are not, however, forced to go to such lengths of doubt in his case as Aristotle did in the case of

Orpheus, denying that such a man ever existed; for though there was a time (particularly in Germany) of skepticism as to that possibility, there is now almost unanimous verdict in favor of the historical reality of the author of the Iliad and the Odyssey. Not that any reliance is to be placed on the details of the old Greek lives of Homer, which are manifestly fictitious; but the internal evidence of the epics themselves leads to the belief in an authorship such as agrees substantially with the kernel from which these very ancient legendary traditions were developed. The central fact in which all these traditions agree is, that the author of these poems was an Asiatic Greek; and though other places are named, the greatest amount of legendary evidence clearly points to Smyrna as the city of Homer's birth. The dialect in which the Iliad and Odyssey are written -- the Ionic -- is the very variety of Greek which was afterwards used in the same region by Herodotus, the father of history, and Hippocrates, the first and greatest of Greek physicians; and the allusions to natural phenomena, especially the frequent mention of the strong nortwest wind blowing from Thrace, plainly indicate the west coast of Asia Minor as the familiar residence of the poet. The chronology of the Homeric poems, both as respects the great central event which they celebrate -- the Trojan War -- and the age of the poet himself, is much more doubtful; but it is quite certain that Homer lived considerably before the recognition of a regularly received record of dates among the Greeks -- that is, before the year 776 BC, the commencement of the calculation by Olympiads. The date given by Herodotus for the age of Homer -- 400 years before his own time, that is, about 850 BC -- is probable enough; but considering the entire want of any reliable foundation for chronology in those early times, we must not seek an accuracy in this matter beyond that which was attained by the Greeks themselves, and allow a free margin of at least 200 years from the time of Solomon (1000 BC) downwards. To throw him further back than the earliest of these dates would be inconsistent at once with the historical elements in the midst of which his poems move; for his epics exhibit characteristics not in keeping with languages at the earliest stages of their literary development. The Ionic dialect used by Homer is, in fact, a highly cultivated shoot of the old Hellenic stock, and which was in the poet's hands so perfect for the highest poetical purposes as to have remained the model for the epic style during the whole period of the literature of the Greeks."

(Quote from nndb.com)

CONTENTS

PUBLISHER'S PREFACE
   HYMN TO DEMETER 1

HYMN TO DEMETER

I begin to sing of rich-haired Demeter, awful goddess -- of her and her trim-ankled daughter whom Aidoneus [Hades] rapt away, given to him by all-seeing Zeus the loud-thunderer. Apart from Demeter, lady of the golden sword and glorious fruits, she was playing with the deep-bosomed daughters of Oceanus and gathering flowers over a soft meadow, roses and crocuses and beautiful violets, irises also and hyacinths and the narcissus which Earth made to grow at the will of Zeus and to please the Host of Many, to be a snare for the bloom-like girl -- a marvellous, radiant flower. It was a thing of awe whether for deathless gods or mortal men to see: from its root grew a hundred blooms and it smelled most sweetly, so that all wide heaven above and the whole earth and the sea's salt swell laughed for joy. And the girl was amazed and reached out with both hands to take the lovely toy; but the wide-pathed earth yawned there in the plain of Nysa, and the lord, Host of Many, with his immortal horses sprang out upon her -- the Son of Cronos, He who has many names.[1]

He caught her up reluctant on his golden car and bare her away lamenting. Then she cried out shrilly with her voice, calling upon her father, the Son of Cronos, who is most high and excellent. But no one, either of the deathless gods or of mortal men, heard her voice, nor yet the olive-trees bearing rich fruit: only tenderhearted Hecate, bright-coiffed, the daughter of Persaeus,

---

[1] The Greeks feared to name Pluto directly and mentioned him by one of many descriptive titles, such as "Host of Many": compare the Christian use of diabolos or our "Evil One."

heard the girl from her cave, and the lord Helios, Hyperion's bright son, as she cried to her father, the Son of Cronos. But he was sitting aloof, apart from the gods, in his temple where many pray, and receiving sweet offerings from mortal men. So he, that Son of Cronos, of many names, who is Ruler of Many and Host of Many, was bearing her away by leave of Zeus on his immortal chariot -- his own brother's child and all unwilling.

And so long as she, the goddess, yet beheld earth and starry heaven and the strong-flowing sea where fishes shoal, and the rays of the sun, and still hoped to see her dear mother and the tribes of the eternal gods, so long hope calmed her great heart for all her trouble. . . . and the heights of the mountains and the depths of the sea rang with her immortal voice: and her queenly mother heard her.

Bitter pain seized her heart, and she rent the covering upon her divine hair with her dear hands: her dark cloak she cast down from both her shoulders and sped, like a wild-bird, over the firm land and yielding sea, seeking her child. But no one would tell her the truth, neither god nor mortal man; and of the birds of omen none came with true news for her. Then for nine days queenly Deo wandered over the earth with flaming torches in her hands, so grieved that she never tasted ambrosia and the sweet draught of nectar, nor sprinkled her body with water. But when the tenth enlightening dawn had come, Hecate, with a torch in her hands, met her, and spoke to her and told her news:

"Queenly Demeter, bringer of seasons and giver of good gifts, what god of heaven or what mortal man has rapt away Persephone and pierced with sorrow your dear heart? For I heard her voice, yet saw not with my eyes who it was. But I tell you truly and shortly all I know."

So, then, said Hecate. And the daughter of rich-haired Rhea answered her not, but sped swiftly with her, holding flaming torches in her hands. So they came to Helios, who is watchman of both gods and men, and stood in front of his horses: and the bright goddess enquired of him: "Helios, do you at least regard me, goddess as I am, if ever by word or deed of mine I have cheered your heart and spirit. Through the fruitless air I heard the thrilling cry of my daughter whom I bare, sweet scion of my body and lovely in form, as of one seized violently; though with my eyes I saw nothing. But you -- for with your beams you look down from the bright upper air over all the earth and sea -- tell me truly of my dear child if you have seen her anywhere, what god or mortal man has violently seized her against her will and mine, and so made off."

So said she. And the Son of Hyperion answered her: "Queen Demeter, daughter of rich-haired Rhea, I will tell you the truth; for I greatly reverence and pity you in your grief for your trim-ankled daughter. None other of the deathless gods is to blame, but only cloud-gathering Zeus who gave her to Hades, her father's brother, to be called his buxom wife. And Hades seized her and took her loudly crying in his chariot down to his realm of mist and gloom. Yet, goddess, cease your loud lament and keep not vain anger unrelentingly: Aidoneus, the Ruler of Many, is no unfitting husband among the deathless gods for your child, being our own brother and born of the same stock: also, for honour, he has that third share which he received when division was made at the first and is appointed lord of those among whom he dwells."

So he spake, and called to his horses: and at his chiding they quickly whirled the swift chariot along, like long-winged birds.

But grief yet more terrible and savage came into the heart of Demeter, and thereafter she was so angered with the dark-clouded Son of Cronos that she avoided the gathering of the gods and high Olympus, and went to the towns and rich fields of men, disfiguring her form a long while. And no one of men or deep-bosomed women knew her when they saw her, until she came to the house of wise Celeus who then was lord of fragrant Eleusis. Vexed in her dear heart, she sat near the wayside by the Maiden Well, from which the women of the place were used to draw water, in a shady place over which grew an olive shrub. And she was like an ancient woman who is cut off from childbearing and the gifts of garland-loving Aphrodite, like the nurses of king's children who deal justice, or like the house-keepers in their echoing halls. There the daughters of Celeus, son of Eleusis, saw her, as they coming for easy-drawn water, to carry it in pitchers of bronze to their dear father's house: four were they and like goddesses in the flower of their girlhood, Callidice and Cleisidice and lovely Demo and Callithoe who was the eldest of them all. They knew her not, -- for the gods are not easily discerned by mortals --, but startling near by her spoke winged words:

"Old mother, whence are you of folk born long ago? Why are you gone away from the city and do not draw near the houses? For there in the shady halls are women of just such age as you, and others younger; and they would welcome you both by word and by deed."

Thus they said. And she, that queen among goddesses answered them saying: "Hail, dear children, whosoever you are of woman-kind. I will tell you my story; for it is not unseemly that I should tell you truly what you ask. Doso is my name, for my stately mother gave it me. And now I am come from Crete over the sea's wide back, -- not willingly; but pirates brought me thence by force of strength against my liking. Afterwards they put in with their swift craft to Thoricus, and these the women landed on the shore in full throng and the men likewise, and they began to make ready a meal by the stern-cables of the ship. But my heart craved not pleasant food, and I fled secretly across the dark country and escaped my masters, that they should not take me unpurchased across the sea, there to win a price for me. And so I wandered and am come here: and I know not at all what land this is or what people are in it. But may all those who dwell on Olympus give you husbands and birth of children as parents desire, so you take pity on me, maidens, and show me this clearly that I may learn, dear children, to the house of what man and woman I may go, to work for them cheerfully at such tasks as belong to a woman of my age. Well could I nurse a new born child, holding him in my arms, or keep house, or spread my masters' bed in a recess of the well-built chamber, or teach the women their work."

So said the goddess. And straightway the unwed maiden Callidice, goodliest in form of the daughters of Celeus, answered her and said:

"Mother, what the gods send us, we mortals bear perforce, although we suffer; for they are much stronger than we. But now I will teach you clearly, telling you the names of men who have great power and honour here and are chief among the people, guarding our city's coif of towers by their wisdom and true judgements: there is wise Triptolemus and Dioclus and Polyxeinus and blameless Eumolpus and Dolichus and our own brave father. All these have wives who manage in the house, and no one of them, so soon as she had seen you, would dishonour you and turn you from the house, but they will welcome you; for indeed you are godlike. But if you will, stay here; and we will go to our father's house and tell Metaneira, our deep-bosomed mother, all this matter fully, that she may bid you rather come to our home than search after the houses of others. She has an only son, late-born, who is being nursed in our well-built house, a child of many prayers and welcome: if you could bring him up until he reached the full measure of youth, any one of womankind who should see you would straightway envy you, such gifts would our mother give for his upbringing."

So she spake: and the goddess bowed her head in assent. And they filled their shining vessels with water and carried them off rejoicing. Quickly they came to their father's great house and straightway told their mother according as they had heard and seen. Then she bade them go with all speed and invite the stranger to come for a measureless hire. As hinds or heifers in spring time, when sated with pasture, bound about a meadow, so they, holding up the folds of their lovely garments, darted down the hollow path, and their hair like a crocus flower streamed about their shoulders. And they found the good goddess near the wayside where they had left her before, and led her to the house of their dear father. And she walked behind, distressed in her dear heart, with her head veiled and wearing a dark cloak which waved about the slender feet of the goddess.

Soon they came to the house of heaven-nurtured Celeus and went through the portico to where their queenly mother sat by a pillar of the close-fitted roof, holding her son, a tender scion, in her bosom. And the girls ran to her. But the goddess walked to the threshold: and her head reached the roof and she filled the doorway with a heavenly radiance. Then awe and reverence and pale fear took hold of Metaneira, and she rose up from her couch before Demeter, and bade her be seated. But Demeter, bringer of seasons and giver of perfect gifts, would not sit upon the bright couch, but stayed silent with lovely eyes cast down until careful Iambe placed a jointed seat for her and threw over it a silvery fleece. Then she sat down and held her veil in her hands before her face. A long time she sat upon the stool[1] without speaking because of her sorrow, and greeted no one by word or by sign, but rested, never smiling, and tasting neither food nor drinks because she pined with longing for her deep-bosomed daughter, until careful Iambe -- who pleased her moods in aftertime also -- moved the holy lady with many a quip and jest to smile and laugh and cheer her heart. Then Metaneira filled a cup with sweet wine and offered it to her; but she refused it, for she said it was not lawful for her to drink red wine, but bade them mix meal and water with soft mint and give her to drink. And Metaneira mixed the draught and gave it to the goddess as she bade. So the great queen Deo received it to observe the sacrament.[2]

And of them all, well-girded Metaneira first began to speak: "Hail, lady! For I think you are not meanly but nobly born; truly dignity and grace are conspicuous upon your eyes as in the eyes of kings that deal justice. Yet we mortals bear per-force what the gods send us, though we be grieved; for a yoke is set upon our necks. But now, since you are come here, you shall have what I can bestow: and nurse me this child whom the gods gave me in my old age and beyond my hope, a son much prayed for. If you should bring him up until he reach the full measure of youth, any one of woman-kind that sees you will straightway envy you, so great reward would I give for his upbringing."

---

[1] Demeter chooses the lowlier seat, supposedly as being more suitable to her assumed condition, but really because in her sorrow she refuses all comforts.

[2] An act of communion -- the drinking of the potion (kykeon) here described -- was one of the most important pieces of ritual in the Eleusinian mysteries, as commemorating the sorrows of the goddess.

Then rich-haired Demeter answered her: "And to you, also, lady, all hail, and may the gods give you good! Gladly will I take the boy to my breast, as you bid me, and will nurse him. Never, I ween, through any heedlessness of his nurse shall witchcraft hurt him nor yet the Undercutter: for I know a charm far stronger than the Woodcutter, and I know an excellent safeguard against woeful witchcraft."[1]

When she had so spoken, she took the child in her fragrant bosom with her divine hands: and his mother was glad in her heart. So the goddess nursed in the palace Demophoon, wise Celeus' goodly son whom well-girded Metaneira bare. And the child grew like some immortal being, not fed with food nor nourished at the breast: for by day rich-crowned Demeter would anoint him with ambrosia as if he were the offspring of a god and breathe sweetly upon him as she held him in her bosom. But at night she would hide him like a brand in the heart of the fire, unknown to his dear parents. And it wrought great wonder in these that he grew beyond his age; for he was like the gods face to face. And she would have made him deathless and unaging, had not well-girded Metaneira in her heedlessness kept watch by night from her sweet-smelling chamber and spied. But she wailed and smote her two hips, because she feared for her son and was greatly distraught in her heart; so she lamented and uttered winged words:

"Demophoon, my son, the strange woman buries you deep in fire and works grief and bitter sorrow for me."

Thus she spoke, mourning. And the bright goddess, lovely-crowned Demeter, heard her, and was wroth with her. So with

---

[1] Undercutter and Woodcutter are probably popular names (after the style of Hesiod's "Boneless One") for the worm thought to be the cause of teething and toothache.

her divine hands she snatched from the fire the dear son whom Metaneira had born unhoped-for in the palace, and cast him from her to the ground; for she was terribly angry in her heart. Forthwith she said to well-girded Metaneira:

"Witless are you mortals and dull to foresee your lot, whether of good or evil, that comes upon you. For now in your heedlessness you have wrought folly past healing; for -- be witness the oath of the gods, the relentless water of Styx -- I would have made your dear son deathless and unaging all his days and would have bestowed on him ever-lasting honour, but now he can in no way escape death and the fates. Yet shall unfailing honour always rest upon him, because he lay upon my knees and slept in my arms. But, as the years move round and when he is in his prime, the sons of the Eleusinians shall ever wage war and dread strife with one another continually. Lo! I am that Demeter who has share of honour and is the greatest help and cause of joy to the undying gods and mortal men. But now, let all the people build me a great temple and an altar below it and beneath the city and its sheer wall upon a rising hillock above Callichorus. And I myself will teach my rites, that hereafter you may reverently perform them and so win the favour of my heart."

When she had so said, the goddess changed her stature and her looks, thrusting old age away from her: beauty spread round about her and a lovely fragrance was wafted from her sweet-smelling robes, and from the divine body of the goddess a light shone afar, while golden tresses spread down over her shoulders, so that the strong house was filled with brightness as with lightning. And so she went out from the palace.

And straightway Metaneira's knees were loosed and she remained speechless for a long while and did not remember to take up her late-born son from the ground. But his sisters heard his pitiful wailing and sprang down from their well-spread beds: one of them took up the child in her arms and laid him in her bosom, while another revived the fire, and a third rushed with soft feet to bring their mother from her fragrant chamber. And they gathered about the struggling child and washed him, embracing him lovingly; but he was not comforted, because nurses and handmaids much less skillful were holding him now.

All night long they sought to appease the glorious goddess, quaking with fear. But, as soon as dawn began to show, they told powerful Celeus all things without fail, as the lovely-crowned goddess Demeter charged them. So Celeus called the countless people to an assembly and bade them make a goodly temple for rich-haired Demeter and an altar upon the rising hillock. And they obeyed him right speedily and harkened to his voice, doing as he commanded. As for the child, he grew like an immortal being.

Now when they had finished building and had drawn back from their toil, they went every man to his house. But golden-haired Demeter sat there apart from all the blessed gods and stayed, wasting with yearning for her deep-bosomed daughter. Then she caused a most dreadful and cruel year for mankind over the all-nourishing earth: the ground would not make the seed sprout, for rich-crowned Demeter kept it hid. In the fields the oxen drew many a curved plough in vain, and much white barley was cast upon the land without avail. So she would have destroyed the whole race of man with cruel famine and have robbed them who dwell on Olympus of their glorious right of gifts and sacrifices, had not Zeus perceived and marked this in his heart. First he sent golden-winged Iris to call rich-haired Demeter, lovely in form. So he commanded. And she obeyed the dark-clouded Son of Cronos, and sped with swift feet across the space between. She came to the stronghold of fragrant

Eleusis, and there finding dark-cloaked Demeter in her temple, spake to her and uttered winged words:

"Demeter, father Zeus, whose wisdom is everlasting, calls you to come join the tribes of the eternal gods: come therefore, and let not the message I bring from Zeus pass unobeyed."

Thus said Iris imploring her. But Demeter's heart was not moved. Then again the father sent forth all the blessed and eternal gods besides: and they came, one after the other, and kept calling her and offering many very beautiful gifts and whatever rights she might be pleased to choose among the deathless gods. Yet no one was able to persuade her mind and will, so wroth was she in her heart; but she stubbornly rejected all their words: for she vowed that she would never set foot on fragrant Olympus nor let fruit spring out of the ground, until she beheld with her eyes her own fair-faced daughter.

Now when all-seeing Zeus the loud-thunderer heard this, he sent the Slayer of Argus whose wand is of gold to Erebus, so that having won over Hades with soft words, he might lead forth chaste Persephone to the light from the misty gloom to join the gods, and that her mother might see her with her eyes and cease from her anger. And Hermes obeyed, and leaving the house of Olympus, straightway sprang down with speed to the hidden places of the earth. And he found the lord Hades in his house seated upon a couch, and his shy mate with him, much reluctant, because she yearned for her mother. But she was afar off, brooding on her fell design because of the deeds of the blessed gods. And the strong Slayer of Argus drew near and said:

"Dark-haired Hades, ruler over the departed, father Zeus bids me bring noble Persephone forth from Erebus unto the gods, that her mother may see her with her eyes and cease from her dread anger with the immortals; for now she plans an awful deed, to destroy the weakly tribes of earthborn men by keeping seed hidden beneath the earth, and so she makes an end of the honours of the undying gods. For she keeps fearful anger and does not consort with the gods, but sits aloof in her fragrant temple, dwelling in the rocky hold of Eleusis."

So he said. And Aidoneus, ruler over the dead, smiled grimly and obeyed the behest of Zeus the king. For he straightway urged wise Persephone, saying:

"Go now, Persephone, to your dark-robed mother, go, and feel kindly in your heart towards me: be not so exceedingly cast down; for I shall be no unfitting husband for you among the deathless gods, that am own brother to father Zeus. And while you are here, you shall rule all that lives and moves and shall have the greatest rights among the deathless gods: those who defraud you and do not appease your power with offerings, reverently performing rites and paying fit gifts, shall be punished for evermore."

When he said this, wise Persephone was filled with joy and hastily sprang up for gladness. But he on his part secretly gave her sweet pomegranate seed to eat, taking care for himself that she might not remain continually with grave, dark-robed Demeter. Then Aidoneus the Ruler of Many openly got ready his deathless horses beneath the golden chariots And she mounted on the chariot and the strong Slayer of Argus took reins and whip in his dear hands and drove forth from the hall, the horses speeding readily. Swiftly they traversed their long course, and neither the sea nor river-waters nor grassy glens nor mountain-peaks checked the career of the immortal horses, but they clave the deep air above them as they went. And Hermes brought them to the place where rich-crowned Demeter was staying and checked them before her fragrant temple.

And when Demeter saw them, she rushed forth as does a Maenad down some thick-wooded mountain, while Persephone on the other side, when she saw her mother's sweet eyes, left the chariot and horses, and leaped down to run to her, and falling upon her neck, embraced her. But while Demeter was still holding her dear child in her arms, her heart suddenly misgave her for some snare, so that she feared greatly and ceased fondling her daughter and asked of her at once: "My child, tell me, surely you have not tasted any food while you were below? Speak out and hide nothing, but let us both know. For if you have not, you shall come back from loathly Hades and live with me and your father, the dark-clouded Son of Cronos and be honoured by all the deathless gods; but if you have tasted food, you must go back again beneath the secret places of the earth, there to dwell a third part of the seasons every year: yet for the two parts you shall be with me and the other deathless gods. But when the earth shall bloom with the fragrant flowers of spring in every kind, then from the realm of darkness and gloom thou shalt come up once more to be a wonder for gods and mortal men. And now tell me how he rapt you away to the realm of darkness and gloom, and by what trick did the strong Host of Many beguile you?"

Then beautiful Persephone answered her thus: "Mother, I will tell you all without error. When luck-bringing Hermes came, swift messenger from my father the Son of Cronos and the other Sons of Heaven, bidding me come back from Erebus that you might see me with your eyes and so cease from your anger and fearful wrath against the gods, I sprang up at once for joy; but he secretly put in my mouth sweet food, a pomegranate seed, and forced me to taste against my will. Also I will tell how he rapt me away by the deep plan of my father the Son of Cronos and carried me off beneath the depths of the earth, and will relate the whole matter as you ask. All we were playing in a lovely meadow, Leucippe and Phaeno and Electra and Ianthe, Melita also and Iache with Rhodea and Callirhoe and Melobosis and Tyche and Ocyrhoe, fair as a flower, Chryseis, Ianeira, Acaste and Admete and Rhodope and Pluto and charming Calypso; Styx too was there and Urania and lovely Galaxaura with Pallas who rouses battles and Artemis delighting in arrows.[1] We were playing and gathering sweet flowers in our hands, soft crocuses mingled with irises and hyacinths, and rose-blooms and lilies, marvellous to see, and the narcissus which the wide earth caused to grow yellow as a crocus. That I plucked in my joy; but the earth parted beneath, and there the strong lord, the Host of Many, sprang forth and in his golden chariot he bore me away, all unwilling, beneath the earth: then I cried with a shrill cry. All this is true, sore though it grieves me to tell the tale."

So did they then, with hearts at one, greatly cheer each the other's soul and spirit with many an embrace: their hearts had relief from their griefs while each took and gave back joyousness.

Then bright-coiffed Hecate came near to them, and often did she embrace the daughter of holy Demeter: and from that time the lady Hecate was minister and companion to Persephone.

And all-seeing Zeus sent a messenger to them, rich-haired Rhea, to bring dark-cloaked Demeter to join the families of the gods: and he promised to give her what rights she should choose among the deathless gods and agreed that her daughter should

---

[1] The list of names is taken -- with five additions -- from Hesiod, Theogony 349 ff.

go down for the third part of the circling year to darkness and gloom, but for the two parts should live with her mother and the other deathless gods. Thus he commanded. And the goddess did not disobey the message of Zeus; swiftly she rushed down from the peaks of Olympus and came to the plain of Rharus, rich, fertile corn-land once, but then in nowise fruitful, for it lay idle and utterly leafless, because the white grain was hidden by design of trim-ankled Demeter. But afterwards, as spring-time waxed, it was soon to be waving with long ears of corn, and its rich furrows to be loaded with grain upon the ground, while others would already be bound in sheaves. There first she landed from the fruitless upper air: and glad were the goddesses to see each other and cheered in heart. Then bright-coiffed Rhea said to Demeter:

"Come, my daughter; for far-seeing Zeus the loud-thunderer calls you to join the families of the gods, and has promised to give you what rights you please among the deathless gods, and has agreed that for a third part of the circling year your daughter shall go down to darkness and gloom, but for the two parts shall be with you and the other deathless gods: so has he declared it shall be and has bowed his head in token. But come, my child, obey, and be not too angry unrelentingly with the dark-clouded Son of Cronos; but rather increase forthwith for men the fruit that gives them life."

So spake Rhea. And rich-crowned Demeter did not refuse but straightway made fruit to spring up from the rich lands, so that the whole wide earth was laden with leaves and flowers. Then she went, and to the kings who deal justice, Triptolemus and Diocles, the horse-driver, and to doughty Eumolpus and Celeus, leader of the people, she showed the conduct of her rites and taught them all her mysteries, to Triptolemus and Polyxeinus and Diocles also, -- awful mysteries which no one may in any way transgress or pry into or utter, for deep awe of the gods checks the voice. Happy is he among men upon earth who has seen these mysteries; but he who is uninitiate and who has no part in them, never has lot of like good things once he is dead, down in the darkness and gloom.

But when the bright goddess had taught them all, they went to Olympus to the gathering of the other gods. And there they dwell beside Zeus who delights in thunder, awful and reverend goddesses. Right blessed is he among men on earth whom they freely love: soon they do send Plutus as guest to his great house, Plutus who gives wealth to mortal men.

And now, queen of the land of sweet Eleusis and sea-girt Paros and rocky Antron, lady, giver of good gifts, bringer of seasons, queen Deo, be gracious, you and your daughter all beauteous Persephone, and for my song grant me heart-cheering substance. And now I will remember you and another song also.

www.ingramcontent.com/pod-product-compliance
Lightning Source LLC
Chambersburg PA
CBHW051607010526
44119CB00056B/813